First of all Joyce Johnson is brilliant! And she works hard too. The perfect success combo. This book is long overdue. Why because education is broken and this book will help fix it. Sales is the engine that drives every company, however we have college kids wandering around campus clueless about their future and career and they don't know much about sales careers or even the how tos of selling. A huge problem for companies that need talented sales teams and need new sales reps to hit the ground running. This book will change the game on sales.

—**Walter Bond**
Author, Retired NBA Player,
& Hall of Fame Motivational Speaker

Top Jobs! Top Earning$

WHY SALES FOR COLLEGE STUDENTS

JOYCE JOHNSON

www.selfpublishn30days.com

Published by Self Publish -N- 30 Days

Copyright 2017 Why Sales For College Students

All rights reserved worldwide. No part of this book may be reproduced or transmitted in any form or by any means electronic or mechanical, including photocopying, recording or by any information storage and retrieval system without written permission from Joyce Johnson and Joyce Johnson Enterprises

Printed in the United States of America
ISBN: 978-1979817042

1. Sales 2. Student Success
Joyce Johnson: Joyce Johnson Enterprises

Disclaimer/Warning: This book is intended for lecture and entertainment purposes only. The author or publisher does not guarantee that anyone following these steps will be a successful business leader. The author and publisher shall have neither liability responsibility to anyone with respect to any loss or damage cause, or alleged to be caused, directly or indirectly by the information contained in this book.

ACKNOWLEDGMENTS

So many people have invested in my life, past, and future. They say it takes a village and I've certainly had one every step of the way. I can't mention everyone which is why I tell you I love you and appreciate you along the way. A big thanks to my family, friends, and mentors who have invested in my life.

My Mother, Patricia Toliver, I have often said I thank God for you because he could have put anyone in charge of me but he gave me you. For that, I am grateful and feel extremely blessed. My siblings Ervin, Rodney, and Yolanda (Shelly), you bring me joy, support, and more love than I can hold. I hope you've felt the love I have for you. The extended siblings, the cousins I love you and I'm proud to know such a giving, loving, smart, and passionate group of individuals. We are family and friends.

My fabulous, amazing Aunts Mabel, Elizabeth (Marie), Lillian, and Rachel. Wow, you women bring everything to the table! I want to be each of you wrapped in one when I grow up.

As the first born grandchild, I shared a special relationship with both my maternal and paternal grandparents. So many lessons, I hope to someday share.

They along with my father, step-father, and uncles are now my angels, thank you.

Bridgette Collins, I have watched and I'm inspired by your ability to passionately pursue your dreams. You once said to me, "Don't talk about it, be about it." As simple as a statement that may seem, it poked me in my gut and sticks with me whenever I second guess my talent, which happens more than I would like to admit. Thank you for your friendship and mentorship.

My nieces Chalise, Erin, Kennedy, and my Godchildren Bryant, LaTara, and Leslie, for you I wake up and work at being the best me. I hope this book inspires you to be great at whatever your heart desires. I love you with my whole heart. To all of the youth in my family, I expect great things and I hope this body of work will open doors to give you a better future. I love each of you.

My personal college mentors and support system that are still my biggest cheerleaders today; DeBorah Thigpen, Bobrie Jefferson Benton, and Paula Marshall Phillips, my heart is full. Thank you for everything and you know what everything is!

My publishing coach, Darren Palmer – God sent me an angel. I'm grateful to have met you.

INTRODUCTION

When I learned that I would graduate from college a year early, an instant panic of what's next struck me. I recall my peers in engineering and nursing being interviewed by companies that visited the campus to recruit them. However, there were no companies or lines at the career fair interviewing students in the communications department (my undergraduate studies). Fast forward XX years college's career placement departments are focusing more on the student body at large. As a result, companies and organizations are now visiting campuses to recruit for all departments including sales. Many sales programs are now available at the undergraduate level. However, many individuals are still unclear of what sales is and hesitant to enter a sales career.

The sales profession has opened so many doors for me; introductions to people with diverse backgrounds and skill sets, organizations, and travel that have contributed to shaping who I am today. This book is my commitment to share information and insight about sales to virtually mentor and contribute to the development of college students.

In 2009 – 2011, after the crash of the mortgage/financial/real estate markets, I read about unemployed college graduates who moved home to the rooms they grew up in while waiting for engineering or jobs with banks, insurance, and other financial entities. In 2013, hope was once again ripped from the enthusiastic college students preparing to graduate and work for top oil and gas companies. I felt their pain because I know that their college career resource team probably had not exposed them to sales opportunities that match their skill set or interest.

This book is a guide for you (the college student) and your parents to understand the foundation of sales, how you currently use sales in your day to day activities, and what transferable skills you have that will help secure a job in any industry. This book will provide direction that most parents and professors cannot due to their lack of knowledge and resources available to the sales profession. I have shared information and experiences to help students understand how you fit in any industry as a sales representative. If you don't get into medical school, there's a sales job for you. If you don't get that engineering job you dreamed of, the sales profession welcomes you. Holding out for a position in media, again there is a sales opportunity for you.

When I attended college, each student was required to enroll into a speech class. I recommend a speech class rewrite to include an introduction to sales. I believe if students understand the art of selling, they would feel a stronger sense of security as graduation approaches. Chapters will include information on types of sales jobs, sales earnings, and how to connect the dots. When you close this book, I want you to feel empowered about your decision to take on an opportunity in sales and know you are about to experience something great!

TABLE OF **CONTENTS**

1. What is Sales 1
2. Sales Roles 11
3. Why Sales for College Students 23
4. Do You Have What It Takes 33
5. Preparation is Key 43
6. Hidden Sales Roles 53
7. How You Get Paid 63
8. What Your Peers Think 73

Closing 81
Appendix A 82
About the Author 85

"All Success begins with the ability to sell something, whether it's a shirt or an idea."

—**Mark Burnett**

CHAPTER 1

WHAT IS SALES?

There are so many myths and scary sales stories, so I understand why some people are reluctant to enter the world of sales. As I searched a definition online to share in this chapter, the descriptions scared me. After reading over the below definitions found on "Merriam-Webster" online, I thought, "No wonder people are afraid of sales." There's a reference to treason, betrayal, selfishness, and the devil in the first three descriptions. No wonder college students are afraid of accepting a sales job after graduation. Have no fear, Aunt Joyce is here to share the truth about sales.

> Definition of SELL
>
> Sold – selling   /   Transitive verb
>
> 1. To deliver or give up in a violations of duty, trust, or loyalty and especially for personal gain: Betray – often used with out – Sell out their country
>
> 2. a: (1) to give up (property) to another for something of value (such as money) (2): to offer for sale
> b: to give up in return for something else especially foolishly or dishonorably – sold his birthright for a mess of pottage
> c: to exact a price for – sold their lives dearly
>
> 3. a: to deliver into slavery for money
> b: to give into power of another – sold his soul to the devil
> c: to deliver the personal service for money

Honestly, these definitions reminded me of my first outside sales job after college selling alarm systems to businesses. Since I graduated early, my roommate moved back to campus, and I rented a one bedroom townhouse in the city. I was terrified but hopeful. Graduation took place in August. In the midst of a hot Texas summer with 90 plus degrees temperatures daily, I had been interviewing for over a month (realizing now that's not a long time) and grew anxious and a little embarrassed that I hadn't found a full-time job. So when I received the contract sales offer, I prematurely quit my commission sales job in the shoe department of a big box store where I was actually earning a decent pay and invested money from my graduation gifts to pay my own way to train in Dallas. I didn't have much money left, so I had to make this work. I think the training was three days, we studied everything there was to know about the alarm system, was given a book to log our customer visits and sent home. The company promised that I would have a manager in the Houston market to assist my first month (which didn't happen). The first couple of weeks I had fire in the belly thinking about the many deals I would close and of course the commission payout. I got up every morning and dressed in my best professional outfit, drove to one shopping center then the next and knocked on doors pitching this new product. Every evening, I would think about the people I met and how I was going to close them. As the No's and not Now's grew, I began to feel discouraged. The following three to four weeks I convinced myself to keep going. Week after week, I spent less time on the field and quit before the 90-day unpaid trial ended. Again, not realizing a month wasn'ta long time. I felt awful and thought to myself that I had failed. It was painful because after graduating I expected so much. Based on what I read, I knew I would be a good salesperson and earn a great salary to help out with my siblings. After all, I had completed my Bachelor's degree. Wasn't graduation the key to success and securing the best job ever? I dusted myself off, pursued another opportunity in the public sector that stared that December, but eventually made my way back to sales. I'm so grateful I stuck with the sales profession and have many great positive stories to share with you.

Let's start with my personal definition of sales. Sales is the art of listening and building relationships that gain trust between individuals while discussing a need, allowing one to inform and educate the other about his/her product or service (solution) and agreeing on an exchange through a form of payment or results. Much better, what the other definitions were missing is the human factor. Sales is all about people and building relationships. Do you have any relationships? Friends, sorority sisters, team members, roommate, campus clubs or organizations you participate in? If so, you are selling every day. Think about it.

Have you ever run for an office? Student council? Class president? What steps did you take to win? How did you prepare to win over your voters? Often I've said, the President of the United States is the number one salesperson in the world! Use my definition of sales to evaluate a candidate's process to win over millions of voters. He and his staff must listen to the public in order to assess the needs of the majority of the population. Once they understand what's at stake, the future President must then begin to build relationships to inform and educate voters on his agenda to fill their needs. If successful at closing the deal, the voters will elect him as their leader. Was that the path you took when running for office? Did you sell the target audience on your offer to serve them?

It's not my goal to simplify the sales process but to relate it to a real experience you've had as a high school or college student as a result of selling. Remember the movie "The Social Network" about Facebook founder, Mark Zuckerberg? Wow, I just realized that was 2010. You were very young. It's a recommended watch as you may have to pitch your own idea someday. The movie covers other points of betrayal and partying but try to stay focused on the selling points.

How did your last job interview go? Never mind. That is another book. Seriously, study your interviewing style, relate it to sales and make adjustments.

Put the book down for a minute. I want you to think about the last time you presented information to persuade an audience to buy something or vote for your project. Not the girls' scout cookie sale. Let's face it, cute kids, cookies, it's a no-brainer. Guys not who's going in to buy the beer. Well, wait that may qualify. Think along the lines of a presentation that required you to communicate information and educate a parent, teachers or class members to make a decision to accept or allow you to move forward. Remember when you convinced your mom it was safe for you to attend an overnight program or sleepover. You sold her on it by informing her of the activity and educating her on every important point; number of adults present, what you would learn, and most important, your best friend's parents said yes. Then you went in for the close and gave them the permission slip to sign.

Write down your best sale ever.

_____

How did it make you feel?

_____

Would you like to feel like that every day?

_____

Why? _____

The interaction of sales allows you to reinvent yourself in every way. If you care about and respect people of all cultures and personalities, have a strong competitive nature or enjoy figuring out the best solution to deliver the best results, there is a sales opportunity for you. Continue reading.

JOYCE **JOHNSON**

WHY SALES FOR COLLEGE STUDENTS

JOYCE **JOHNSON**

WHY SALES FOR COLLEGE STUDENTS

JOYCE **JOHNSON**

WHY SALES FOR COLLEGE STUDENTS

JOYCE **JOHNSON**

WHY SALES FOR COLLEGE STUDENTS

CHAPTER 2
SALES ROLES

Wow, you decided to venture on to this chapter. Hmm, I think you're hooked. Don't worry, it's not like the broken heart of high school love but more like your first ride at Disney World. You're probably thinking, "I think I can sell, but I need to know a little more." You're right. You need a general understanding of what the sales role requires and how to align your strengths. You have probably worked a couple of jobs by now. What did you like the most about each job? Do you like selling to an individual (students in the bookstore) or door to door? Do you prefer to work on the phones like when calling potential voters or asking for donations? How about inbound calls when you respond to customers' questions and assist with placing orders? If you haven't worked in an area of interest, talk to a friend or family member that have. Write down three to four questions you would like to know about their experiences. It's important to dig deeper to answer the questions above. WHY? Because there are two types of sellers; a Hunter and a Farmer! Let's talk about the Hunter role first.

THE HUNTER

There's an old tale often seen on motivational posters about the Lion, King of the Jungle. The story goes, "Every morning in Africa, the gazelle wakes up and knows it must outrun the fastest Lion or it will be killed. Every morning a Lion wakes up and knows it has to outrun the slowest Gazelle or it will starve to death." It doesn't matter if you're a Lion or Gazelle, when the sun comes up you better be running. The Hunter is the Lion. He hunts to eat!

The Hunter's role is to identify companies that can benefit from their company's products or service. The hunter must make calls and/or knock on doors daily. Once an opportunity is uncovered, the hunter must verify the need by getting in to see the right contact/influencer or decision maker and inform he or she about his offer to get their buy-in or agreement that there is a need. Once the hunter truly understands what the customer needs, the hunter creates a presentation to educate the decision maker how his offer meets the needs of their organization. Once the customer agrees, the hunter asks for the business and closes the deal. Then he eats!

Sales moves at a very fast pace. It requires a relentless work ethic. Get up and run daily.

THE FARMER

What comes to mind when you hear the word "farmer?" Does it take you to photos of a farm and what daily chores are required to keep the farm running? Vision the beautiful fields of crops you see when driving down a rural road. If you look far enough back, you see workers watching over the land, clearing any debris, watering it and keeping out any animal's or bug's interest in feeding off the land. That's the farmer's role. Your responsibility is to take over an existing body of business (customer base) previously sold or contracted by the Hunter. You're responsible for following up with the customer, add on sales, and working through any issues while providing exceptional customer service. You are required to retain the customer and grow their relationship/revenue with your company.

The farmer cares for and hunts within the land he or she protects.

INSIDE / OUTSIDE SALES ROLES

Now that sales is on your radar, you will begin to read ads and have additional questions about the job descriptions. One question for sure will be if an inside or outside sales role is best for you. In most cases, inside sales roles includes checking into a location (some virtual) and making (outbound) or accepting (inbound) calls. Outside sales representatives spend some time in the office making follow up calls and creating proposals or presentations. However, most of their time is spent in front of potential customers developing business opportunities and closing deals. Both inside and outside sales roles can be considered hunters or farmers.

NETWORK MARKETING

Probably the most misunderstood form of selling is network marketing. Some refer to it as a pyramid scheme. There once was a lot of negative opinions or fear of involvement with network marketing organizations. Network marketing is sales. However, you pay to become a member of the organization. There is then a sales and a recruiting component to generate income. You will be responsible for selling a product or service and building a team by recruiting others into the organization often described as a direct line. Keep in mind that this sales job is considered self-employment\entrepreneurship.

TANGIBLE GOODS VS. NON-TANGIBLE PRODUCTS OR SERVICE

At the time of writing this book, I worked for a company that sells tangible goods. I've also sold non-tangible products/service as I started my sales career in education and moved over to telecommunications, and remember the job after college selling the alarm systems. Tangible is when you have a physical product to deliver to your customers like your Apple Watch or phone. Non-tangible is the data they sell you to talk or send text, you never see it, but you know that it's there.

WHERE DO I BELONG?

How do you know what's the best role for you? Have you ever taken a personality assessment? If so, I recommend that you take some time to review it. Start with your weakness but don't stay on there long. The importance of knowing your weakness is to understand what areas you need to build partnerships or identify good resources to assist you vs areas where you will lead. I took my first assessment when I applied for a job in my 20s. It stated my weakness as allowing issues to build up, then blowing up; instead of addressing them along the way. I knew it was important to make myself uncomfortably aware in that area for the benefit of my professional and personal relationships. I adopted the practice of requesting a meeting with co-workers, boyfriend, and others and communicating the topic of discussion so that they wouldn't be caught off guard. Again, address any significant weakness but apply most of your energy on your strengths and master those. if you are Good at persuading others to see things your way, fast learner, great personality, assertive, and most importantly, not afraid to hear no,you are ready for a sales career. we will discuss a few tools later in the book to help you identify your strengths and transferable skills key to your success in sales.

Remember to do your homework. Take time to have conversations with individuals that work in the profession. If you don't know anyone, go to a local company and ask to intern or talk to a local representative. Also, reach out on social media to ask if a friend is willing to introduce you to someone. Review your options and decide who you want to be, a hunter or farmer. If you choose wrongly, no worries, try the other side.

Happy Selling!

JOYCE **JOHNSON**

WHY SALES FOR COLLEGE STUDENTS

_____

_____

_____

_____

_____

_____

_____

_____

_____

_____

_____

_____

JOYCE **JOHNSON**

WHY SALES FOR COLLEGE STUDENTS

JOYCE **JOHNSON**

WHY SALES FOR COLLEGE STUDENTS

JOYCE **JOHNSON**

WHY SALES FOR COLLEGE STUDENTS

CHAPTER 3

WHY SALES FOR COLLEGE STUDENTS

My major is… it doesn't matter. There is a sales opportunity for you. This is why sales is the best option for you, the college student. Why? Sales is fun, challenging, competitive; yet, flexible. You're not hired for what you know but for what you will learn and create. How well you tell a story that informs, educates, and engages your customer will determine your success.

You may not secure the exact job you desire in your field of study; however, sales offers you the opportunity to stay close to the field and continue learning.

Communications or media relations students, the world is yours! You ask, how do I know? Communications/journalism was my field of study. Here's how I got started. I mentioned my first professional sales experience with the alarm company. You're going to love the second one. I graduated and had several interviews with TV and radio stations but didn't make the cut. After taking a state job, then working for a temp agency as a technical writer for an engineering firm, I responded to a call center job. Initially thinking I would work part-time for a couple of months to save money for a vacation and quit. Things changed when I learned the opportunity posted was to sell Houston Rockets season tickets. You know where I'm going with this.

Months went by as we made calls from a remote location. Then it happened, Rockets ran a promo during an away game to target future season ticket holders. A group of us went over to the arena known then as the Summit and now the well-known Lakewood Church. That night was one of the best and may still make my Top 10 list. Performing that night was the late Sammy Davis Jr. Ok, Google him! We were having a ball, listening to the concert, winning money from the sales contest, but none of it tops what happens next. The general manager of the Rockets walked in and asked, who knew a particular software and typed x amount of words per minute. I raised my hand and was presented with a non-disclosure to sign. I then followed several men to the main office and began to edit a player's contract. Yes, that's right! Afterward, the general manager asked what my goal was. I said, "To work here at the Rockets," and gave my elevator pitch. He said, "Contact my secretary in the morning," and 10 days later I started work with the Houston Rockets. Sales open doors!

Let's talk about a few other majors. A popular sales job that you may be aware of is pharmaceutical or healthcare sales. You ever think about their educational background? I am a member of the National Sales Network, an organization focused on the development of sales professionals and providing opportunities for additional training and networking amongst peers. Many pharmaceutical sales representatives are active in the organization. The industry is known for having the most professionally aggressive sales teams. Curious to understand more about the industry, I engaged in conversations with individuals by inquiring how they got started. The first person I talked to attended College and studied Biology with plans to go to medical school. When his medical school plans didn't iron out, he took a pharmaceutical job in a specialized area of medicine. The sales profession allows you to follow your passion. Interested in pre-natal, work in an area that creates tools or medicine for pre-natal care or premature conditions. You can sell drugs like Viagra to drugs that promote health of AIDS or decrease pain for Cancer patients. Whatever your area of medical or science studies, if you have a passion for curing an illness or for building awareness around an illness, there is a sales opportunity for you. Sales allows you to continue learning on the ground floor to launch your personal platform and to inspire others.

Psychology and sociology majors, you're studying and understand human behavior of individuals and groups. The first key to uncovering and closing a sales deal is to build a rapport with your customer. If you truly understand behaviors, personality or cultures, your skills and insight can lead you to develop successful relationships. Companies spend millions every year training sales teams on the "How To" of building relationships and understand customer engagement. You're currently studying many of the assessments within your program to prepare you to identify personality traits and how best to respond. You should be successful in sales building customer rapport!

Are you an education major? In addition to selling books, educational software, and training programs, many companies have education-focused business sectors. Education is a key vertical market for many

WHY SALES FOR COLLEGE STUDENTS

companies and aligns with your major; primary, secondary, and higher education. As a college student, you may think of education as just going to school and paying tuition, teachers, students, grades. As a future graduate, think of it as a huge business opportunity. Education is a business with a very large annual budget. Begin to walk around campus and educate yourself on the many areas of business. Visit the career development department, investors' affairs, public relations, marketing (Who manages social media?). Introduce your engineering buddies to the maintenance department. You will understand why later. There's a company selling a product or service to each area of business. Before you leave campus, find out what companies are selling to which departments and WHY.

Other vertical markets may include; retail for you fashion majors, oil and gas, technology, finance, real estate (property management), travel, and many others. Government markets may interest political science majors; within government, there are law enforcement for the criminal justice or law majors, city, county, state and federal areas of focus.

Sales is also offered as a field of study at many universities today. You may consider taking a couple of classes as an elective to learn a few basic concepts and gain insight to the WHY of the sales process. Taking a few classes may not guarantee success in the field but remove the fear of myths related to sales. I don't want you to graduate and accept defeat if you don't find that wish job. There's a saying, "When life hands you lemons, you make lemonade." Launching your sales career will be the best lemonade you ever taste!

JOYCE **JOHNSON**

WHY SALES FOR COLLEGE STUDENTS

WHY SALES FOR COLLEGE STUDENTS

JOYCE **JOHNSON**

WHY SALES FOR COLLEGE STUDENTS

JOYCE **JOHNSON**

WHY SALES FOR COLLEGE STUDENTS

CHAPTER 4

DO YOU HAVE WHAT IT TAKES?

*"Success is walking from failure
to failure with no loss of enthusiasm."*
—**Winston Churchill**

Now that you have learned more about sales, what's next? You may be asking yourself, can I do this? Do I have what it takes? You may not know if you have what it takes until you try a job in sales. I recommend asking a few instructors, current employer or friends to share three adjectives that describe your personality or work ethic. However, don't over think it. If you're interested in a sales career, go for it!

I believe that sales professionals share several personality traits. Years ago, as a sales leader, I found myself recruiting in a very competitive market. During a meeting with my sales effectiveness manager, she recommended hosting several open houses onsite. The strategy was to invite potential candidates referred by current employees. Since we had tried most traditional routes; including professional recruiting companies, we decided to give this a try. She sweetened the pie by offering gift cards to employees for bringing a friend.

Two weeks later, I was provided with a guest list and copies of potential candidates' resume. We kicked off the evening with a basic welcome and brief presentation of the company. I began to walk the room and held brief conversations with individuals. Suddenly, this guy I will refer to as Mr. M interrupted my conversation to introduce himself. I couldn't recall reviewing a resume for MR. M but continued to engage in conversation. He presented himself, gave his best elevator pitch; including WHY he was a good fit and asked for the job. We agreed the next step would be an interview. Just in case you're curious, I am sharing this story for you to identify a few characteristics (adjectives) about Mr. M.

Mr. M and I scheduled an interview for the following week. I must point out here to be as flexible as possible when interviewing except if you are currently employed. Employers will respect that you have to schedule early morning or late afternoon after work. That is the work ethic and commitment they are looking for in their next hire. Back to Mr. M. He showed up early (please be minimum 15 minutes early to an interview). I observed his confident interaction with team members. The HR person escorted him in. The first interview was a panel interview with several managers within the organization. Each manager asked two questions and then allowed Mr. M to ask us questions about the company. He was prepared and had done his homework on the company and our leadership team. He answered our questions using examples of his past experiences and related them to our industry. Following the interview, other leaders with team openings focused on Mr. M not having industry experience. Secretly, I knew they would and counted on it. I had made a decision that I wanted him on my team. So next steps.

I had the HR manager schedule a second interview. The next interview was a one on one. I was looking for consistency in his answers around his experience, and the confidence was not arrogance that would crumble under the first cloud of conflict. After spending 45 minutes or so with Mr. M, I shared with him my interest in bringing him aboard. With that said, it was one catch, the only position I had open required a technical assessment, and he didn't have experience in that area. I told him if he passed the technical assessment I would hire him. I handed Mr. M a study guide and gave him two weeks to prepare for the test. Well, you've probably jumped ahead to determine the results. Yes, he passed the assessment within the timeline given and was offered the job. Perseverance is key!

Just tonight following Hurricane Harvey leaving the City of Houston under water, my niece called me upset because her job isn't busy and cut her hours. I could hear in her voice how upset and disappointed she was. A while later I texted her, "Try not to stress, keep your game face on. Cry if you must out of frustration. Then bounce back!" I truly believe the college student is the most resilient generation. You will have a few failures but not enough to run and hide. You may want to and take a very brief break if needed then dust yourself off and go get that job you want!

I have mentored and worked with college students for many years, and they have taught me as much as I have shared with them. I have learned about every new app and software application to simplify procedures through the knowledge or research of a college student. You have a lot to offer an employer, but you must convince yourself first, then do your homework.

WHY SALES FOR COLLEGE STUDENTS

Make sure you take time to prepare for every opportunity. Read this chapter and the experience of Mr. M again. Think about the challenges he had to overcome in order to get the job. What have you experienced in the last four years that you had to overcome? How did you prepare? What research, studying or training was required to succeed in accomplishing your goals? If you haven't challenged yourself to take steps outside of your comfort zone, start now.

I mentioned earlier the importance of taking assessments and spending the time to understand your strength and weakness. Don't over think it because you're young, time and the right mentor will help you develop your talent. Spend time to write down your personal assessment and compare it to the professional one. Self-awareness is important. The earlier you can understand what you are afraid of and why, the sooner you can overcome them. You must kick down the door of fear to cross over to personal success.

Request the feedback, accept the feedback, assess it and take steps to polish your weaknesses and develop your strengths. The time is now to plan your entry into the world. You're in the right place at the right time. Believe there's a sales job for you. College is a training camp for all things possible!

JOYCE **JOHNSON**

WHY SALES FOR COLLEGE STUDENTS

JOYCE **JOHNSON**

WHY SALES FOR COLLEGE STUDENTS

JOYCE **JOHNSON**

WHY SALES FOR COLLEGE STUDENTS

JOYCE **JOHNSON**

WHY SALES FOR COLLEGE STUDENTS

CHAPTER 5

PREPARATION IS KEY!

Be prepared, be prepared, be prepared, I can't say this enough. I'm sure you've heard this statement from your parents, teachers, and coaches. When playing sports you train, practice, and play. When you have a test scheduled you study, you prepare. I have mentored many students; I hope they learned two things, be prepared and adopted one of my favorite sayings, "Put Your Game Face ON! Game face is not reserved for the Big Game but the Biggest Game of all Adulthood."

WHO ARE YOU?

As a sales leader, I tried to select books and activities that would help my team in their professional and personal lives. When using these tools to assess your skill set, strengths, and sometimes weakness, think about how you can benefit by applying the techniques to your personal and professional relationships. Earlier I mentioned that employers might request potential candidates to take a personality assessment. Search, review, and select one that works best for you. It's amazing what you will learn about your strengths and weaknesses. Once you get past the initial shock of the data, commit to being honest with yourself about what you find. Share your results with a parent or someone you trust. STOP here, take an assessment and answer the questions below.

What did you learn about yourself that you were not aware of prior to taking the test?

1. _____

2. _____

Based on the above, what changes do you plan to make?

1. _____

2. _____

Pat yourself on the back for completing this exercise. Going this deep can stir many emotions. You will survive. As you enter the professional workspace,

Self-awareness is essential to help you identify development opportunities and relationships to support your success.

"Knowing yourself is the beginning of all wisdom."
—**Aristotle**

"Knowing how others perceive you is a gift from God."
—**Michelle Thornton Ghee**

THE INTRODUCTION

Now that you have a deeper understanding of who you are, it's time to introduce you to the world, not the high-school-you or the-college-you but the New you. It's time to reinvent yourself into the Professional Powerhouse you wish to be. Below is your preparation checklist of tools needed for a successful job search. You will need;

1. A one-page introduction summary about you – Be creative.
2. Your resume.
3. An elevator pitch. Search the World Wide Web for examples.
4. Collect or confirm three (3) to five (5) references.
5. A LinkedIn profile (scrub all social media).
6. Identify companies in your field of study and connect to someone in Sales.

An introductory summary is like a cover letter. It allows you to add things that are not presented in the resume; personal accomplishments, goals, and special interests of study. They can also be created outside the traditional format.

Some of you may have learned about an elevator pitch for the first time in this book. The concept is that if you meet a person of influence on the elevator, you have 60 seconds to state your name, why he or she should hire you (how you can help their business), and ask for the job. The pitch is also valuable to address that awkward silence when asked, "Tell me about yourself." You should practice your pitch until you can deliver it flawlessly.

Social media. You understand the impact of social media as well as anyone. Employers will search and review profiles. If you have any derogatory post, photos or videos online, I recommend you remove them and/or close your account if needed. Unless you are earning a living promoting your pages, they are not worth the risks.

TIME TO CONNECT

So you made it to college. What have you done to prepare for your future since arriving that summer or fall semester? Do you participate in any campus organizations, volunteer? What type of courses have you taken outside of your major? College campuses are lecture havens hosting diverse individuals speaking on many topics. Begin now to expand your reach to meet students, guests, and professors outside of your degree focus. Attend meet-ups, chamber of commerce, and other professional organizations or events. The goal is to network for a connection. Many people attend events to collect cards. Your goal is to find someone of influence that you have something in common with. The difference is that the connection will remember your name, have their admin send your call through, and refer you to a friend or contact. In addition to new contacts, make a list of existing ones and where they work (hopefully you've kept in touch). Reach out and ask for referral

Follow up to report on your success.

JOYCE **JOHNSON**

READY SET GO!

You are now prepared with the basic tools to get you in the door. Follow up with your school's career center to review your documents and schedule a mock interview. Practice with your friends and family. Be on time to your interview, and yes, wear a navy or black suit (both men and women). Your competition will be ready, so if you take the process lightly, count it as a loss. Remember the story of the Lion and Gazelle and get up running!

I didn't know it was a Sales Job!

JOYCE **JOHNSON**

WHY SALES FOR COLLEGE STUDENTS

JOYCE **JOHNSON**

WHY SALES FOR COLLEGE STUDENTS

JOYCE **JOHNSON**

WHY SALES FOR COLLEGE STUDENTS

JOYCE **JOHNSON**

WHY SALES FOR COLLEGE STUDENTS

CHAPTER 6
HIDDEN SALES ROLES

Have you ever responded to a job ad only to get there and it's a telemarketing sales job? I am willing to bet many of you walked away or declined the offer. I hope what you learn about sales in this chapter will help you identify sales careers and remove the fear of selling so that you can assess the potential opportunity. Remember, if you are offering goods or services in exchange for money or service you are selling.

RECRUITING

As you prepare for graduation, recruiters from many industries will approach you with their "sales" pitch on why their company is the best. Athletes think about the process and approach of scouts to influence you to select the college they represent. You may have friends being recruited by a Sports Agents (sales). Recruiters are paid in some capacity for closing the deal with you. Private recruiting companies are paid by employers to find the best talent match for their job openings. Organizations also have internal recruiting staff, and small business Human Resource teams may hold dual roles. All recruiters have the same responsibility to persuade you that their company, organization or school is the best for you. Yes, recruiting is a sales job.

THE BUSINESS OF SOCIAL MEDIA

Here is an area where you can teach me, and I appreciate any tips you share. Last night, I went online to Nordstrom to look for a jumpsuit. I first noticed the outfit on an Instagram ad. So I logged on to Nordstrom.com then changed my mind. However, Nordstrom is persistent. When I signed on to Facebook, an ad with the jumpsuit was in my personal feed. Are you currently promoting your social media pages or a company's? What are your goals for the pages? Connections? Followers? Why? I think you want to sell them on you. Are you looking for companies to pay you to sell their products to your personal audience? There was a time (before you were born) when companies marketing budget was focused on print, radio, and TV ads until the Internet enabled a new platform of marketing and online sales. I believe online and social media sales will be the most competitive retail sales space.

REAL ESTATE AGENT

Do you know any real estate agents? How many signs do you see when you drive through the neighborhood? Has it sparked your interest? Real estate is one of those industries with high turnover because individuals of all job titles jump in for the flexible schedule and potential income. However, many people do not realize that the job of a real estate agent is an entrepreneur and sales role. The great thing about the industry is most firms have training programs, and you can intern or support an agent while taking certification courses. You are your own boss and must have the discipline and work ethic to focus on generating and closing business. Your skills to build a rapport is important as you need the applicant to sign a letter of intent for you to represent their purchase or sale. The agent then has to sell them on the right house, an offer and negotiate with the seller and their agent on behalf of his customers. It's called a closing when the purchase is made and the seller and buyer exchange keys to their new home. Sales.

JOYCE **JOHNSON**

ENTREPRENEURSHIP

Often peers have shared that they are leaving corporate America to pursue their dreams of self-employment or business ownership. During a recent conversation, a friend shared that she is ready to retire from **sales** to build her own business. I chuckled and commented, "From the fire to the frying pan!" She asked, why that comment. I said, "You will work harder and have to sell more than you ever have because now you are responsible for ensuring the lights turn on when employees show up for work. You begin by selling future partners or investors on your business plan. Once you've secured financing, you need employees, vendor support, and customers.

It's not easy; yet, very fulfilling. I've done it, jumped into self-employment and business ownership. Writing this book is an entrepreneur project. Of course, I thought it was a good idea and an important message. However, that wasn't enough; I had to sell the marketing company and its leaders on the idea. Add hours of writing each day to find the right words to sell you on a sales career. By now I am visiting and following up on every media, PR or marketing opportunity within reach to sell them on why they should share this book with their fans. I'm up early and late working to inform and educate as many students as possible on

WHY SALES FOR COLLEGE STUDENTS

WHY a sales career is best for them. The business of Entrepreneurial Sales!

OTHER SALES CAREERS

As you were reading this chapter, thoughts of offers or companies (recruiters) visiting the college may have come to mind. I hope you're online researching job offers for true sales opportunities. A few that are popular during college career days;

- Financial Adviser
- Loan Officer
- Insurance Agent
- Stock Broker
- Retail Associate
- College Admissions Officers
- Marketing Associated
- Fitness Trainer
- Product vendor

I hope you found this chapter helpful. Contact me on social media @iamjoycejohnson to ask questions or share feedback. Do your homework on job titles. Reach out to people on social media that are currently in the role of interest. Ask for 15 minutes to share their insight. You will be surprised how many will say yes. Be flexible, on time, and respectful. Next, I encourage you to create a list of transferable skills you have that will help land the interview and the job. Consider Sales as an option for you!

JOYCE **JOHNSON**

WHY SALES FOR COLLEGE STUDENTS

JOYCE **JOHNSON**

WHY SALES FOR COLLEGE STUDENTS

JOYCE **JOHNSON**

WHY SALES FOR COLLEGE STUDENTS

JOYCE **JOHNSON**

WHY SALES FOR COLLEGE STUDENTS

CHAPTER 7

HOW YOU GET PAID?

SALES COMPENSATION PACKAGES

"Opportunities are usually disguised as hard work, so most people don't recognize them."
—**Ann Landers**

Most books you read will tell you to follow your love, your passion but if you were doing that we wouldn't be here. Right now, you are searching for money. Money to pay student loans. Money to leave the room you grew up in or not go back to it. Money to travel, party, and have the best apartment in the downtown area of your favorite city with a hot car and hot mate! You may have a bigger responsibility like helping your family rebuild or pay debt, either way, your goal as you prepare for graduation is to follow the money! Sales will work you harder than most careers, drive you to exceed your most aggressive goals, and pay you a higher compensation package than most entry-level jobs. Sales is an opportunity missed hidden behind fear and hard work.

Let's be clear, if it's listed as a sales job and does not offer commissions and/or bonuses plan - walk away. I have accepted opportunities with different types of compensation plans but never one that does not offer incentives. Salespeople live for incentives – money, trips, awards, and yes, even gift cards. I recently shared with someone that I like gift cards, and they made joke of it that I didn't find funny. I once had a flat tire and tipped the college student who came out to fix it with a $25 Chilli's gift card. He had tears in his eyes. I have also used them to tip at the airport. I think I will purchase a few for my next trip. I know people appreciate them as much as I do.

Recently, I was in Los Angeles and invited my younger cousin to join me at the Lakers game. He was there training for his first post-college job. The company is paying for his hotel, food, and gave him a $50 VISA card that day. He was so appreciative. He bought his own food at the game and had credit available to buy gas for his car. He thought that was awesome, and so did I.

There are a variety of compensation plans ultimately you must decide where you feel (yes, follow your intuition) most comfortable and will receive support as someone new to the role. In addition to pay, ask about the training and mentorship programs. It's important you have support or you may grow frustrated and leave prematurely, or worse get fired or give up like I did on my first sales job and default on something not as fulfilling. Don't over think it, just make the best decision within a given timeframe.

SALARY + COMMISSIONS

This payment plan is pretty simple. You receive a base salary and commissions based on reaching communicated sales goals. Yes, commission plans and goals may change some for the better, others not so much. Some commission plans pay out at 100%, others pay by dollars received or multiple targets met. Take time to understand your plan and how to maximize your earnings. I have learned decisions on compensation plans are made well above my pay grade. Your job is to stay focus and to outsell any plan. Stay ahead of your goals. Become a forecasting expert. We will discuss forecasting in the next book. I promise.

DRAW + COMMISSIONS

A draw is a minimum payment an employer will pay you as a ramp up until you build up enough sales to earn commissions or if you do not meet a monthly sales target. There are two types of draw payment plans – recoverable and non-recoverable. Recoverable means the employer will deduct what they have paid you as a draw once you begin earning commissions. Non-recoverable does not require you to pay the funds back. Some companies will pay you a three-month non-recoverable draw to allow you time to close deals. Some companies offer a minimum payout via draws, some require you to pay them back, and others do not. I have several friends in the insurance and financial consultant business that are paid on a draw + commission compensation plan.

COMMISSIONS ONLY

Commission only is just what it says. You are only paid if you sell something. Some companies may offer a draw to ramp up, others will not. In this environment, the payout is normally aggressive to entice you to join the company. Startup companies with small budgets may decide to offer a commission only plan. Companies may also ask you to invest in your sample kit or materials. Most Network

WHY SALES FOR COLLEGE STUDENTS

Marketing companies I've encountered require an initial investment from you.

Real Estate agents, loan officers, title companies, and appraisers are paid under this compensation plan. There may be some companies out there that offer a salary or draw; personally, I haven't heard of them. There are financial institutions that pay their loan officers; however, in most private companies, it is a commission only compensation plan. When paid under commissions only plan, you are normally in a sales roles as an independent contractor. This means you are self-employed, an entrepreneur, even if the company offers training or support, you are independent.

BONUSES/INCENTIVES

Here's where the fun begins. Most people (people run companies) believe that all salespeople are money motivated. The leaders who really get us understand it's not the money but what we can do with it. This is where bonuses and really great incentives kick in. Companies create bonus plans and incentives for top salespeople. I have won prizes like furniture, big screen TV, and again my favorite Amex gift cards. Trips include, Disneyland and World, but my favorite was to Park City, Utah because I took my brother and we had a blast. Anyone who knows me is aware that I prefer warm weather vacations, but that trip was special. I had to threaten to call my mother several times as my brother the daredevil drove around the mountains like he was in a professional race. Priceless. I'm grateful for the experience.

ADDITIONAL BENEFITS

Additional benefits are medical, dental, vision insurance savings, and retirement plans. Some companies form partnerships providing discounts with retail stores, lawyers, auto dealerships, cell phone providers, and more. I have a group of friends in sales roles, and everyone's company offer something different. Take time to review the additional benefits your new company offer. You can save time and money. As we say in sales, time is money.

JOYCE **JOHNSON**

WHY SALES FOR COLLEGE STUDENTS

JOYCE **JOHNSON**

WHY SALES FOR COLLEGE STUDENTS

JOYCE **JOHNSON**

WHY SALES FOR COLLEGE STUDENTS

JOYCE **JOHNSON**

WHY SALES FOR COLLEGE STUDENTS

CHAPTER 8

WHAT YOUR PEERS THINK

Now that you have taken a look into the world of sales, I hope you have a fire of excitement in your belly. Will you pursue a career in sales? Tweet me a response @iamjoycejohnson.

One common feeling of the many students I mentored was "anxiety" towards graduating and finding a job in their field of study. However, they hadn't given the job of interviewing process 100% of the commitment it takes to land the right job. I think the lazybones attitude was due to a couple of myths I would like to address. 1. If you go to college, there will be a job waiting when you graduate. 2. Once you find this perfect job, you <u>will</u> retire with the company. No and no. It's up to you to start your day running!

I have shared what I know and may have intrigued many of you. However, I realize there are still some non-believers. So I asked a few of your peers to share their perspective on the sales profession and the impact on their lives.

Q. How did you learn about the sales profession?

- I learned about sales when I became a personal trainer. In that field, sales is partly selling yourself as well as learning to overcome objections, which I believe is the key to sales.

Q. Were you afraid or hesitant to enter the sales field?

- Although my mom was a top performing sales person and I consider myself a people person, I was afraid. I'm not afraid anymore, but still learning how to inject my bubbly personality when having a business conversation.
- After playing college football in front of 100,000 fans and against Heisman trophy candidates, there was nothing about sales that scared me but finding good tactics and applying best practices was the hard part.

WHY SALES FOR COLLEGE STUDENTS

Q. Did you have any previous sales experience?

- No. Well, maybe I waited tables.
- I sold everything to put myself through college. One summer, I made over $3K in two months selling Cutco knives.
- Before I graduated, I worked in retail. I was hired in an entry level outside sales role after college and promoted after two years.

Q. Has the sales profession met your expectations?

- When it comes to my expectations of workload and compensation, I am satisfied. Being able to control and transform my business and see the benefits from that metrics on my paycheck is a great feeling.
- My expectations were met for my personal goals. Most sales jobs are in some form of commission based. I set my goals and attacked them.
- I married young and was able to buy a house and allow my wife to work part-time to be home with our son.

Q. Was sales a good choice for you? Why?

- It was a good choice for me because I'm a people person and adaptable to any environment. Everyone you come in contact with will not be where you are from, share your interest or point of view.

- Sales was a good choice for me because it challenged me to step outside of my comfort zone. It taught me independence, entrepreneurship, the power of networking, and much more.
- Sales has endless possibilities and room for you to create the ones you want.
- Sales contributed to me becoming an entrepreneur. I learned how to develop my personal brand. I took best practices from companies I worked for and thought what I would do differently to determine the brand I want to sell to my customers.

Q. Any recommendations for your peers?

- At some point you have bought something from someone reverse your role, I think it would be great if my sales person did this or I wish they would have said that.
- Role play with your peers, family, and friends. Practice scenarios so that when faced with an objection it will be easy to respond. Think through the what ifs.

JOYCE **JOHNSON**

WHY SALES FOR COLLEGE STUDENTS

JOYCE **JOHNSON**

WHY SALES FOR COLLEGE STUDENTS

JOYCE **JOHNSON**

WHY SALES FOR COLLEGE STUDENTS

JOYCE **JOHNSON**

WHY SALES FOR COLLEGE STUDENTS

CLOSING

To My College Students With Love,

I set out to help you to determine the best or alternative path for your career. You have heard from me and your peer group about what sales is, the personal development benefits and pay. I believe that sales offers you the best opportunity to stay aligned with your field of study and transition from an inspiring college student to an inspirational adult. I wish you the very best on your journey. **Always be prepared, work hard, play hard, and most importantly, help others!**

Make it a great day! Everyday!

APPENDIX A
NATIONAL SALES PROGRAMS

Check with your college or university to learn if they offer a sales program. Below is a list of programs posted on www.salesfoundation.org. If your campus doesn't have a program, reach out to several of the following, they may offer online courses or virtual programs to support your interest in a sales career.

WHY SALES FOR COLLEGE STUDENTS

NORTH AMERICAN SALES SCHOOLS

Auburn University
Ball State University
Baylor University
Bowling Green University
Bradley University
Bryant University
California State University, Chico
California State University, Fullerton
Central Michigan University
Clemson University
College of New Jersey
Concordia University-St. Paul
DePaul University
Douglas College
Duquesne University
Elon University
Ferris State University
Florida International University
Florida State University
Georgia Southern University
Georgia State University
Illinois State University
Indiana State University
Indiana University
Kansas State University
Kennesaw State University

Michigan State University
Missouri State University
Nicholls State University
North Carolina A&T State University
North Dakota State University
Northern Illinois University
Nova Southeastern University
Ohio University
Plymouth State University
Purdue University
Southern New Hampshire University
Southern University Baton Rouge
St. Catherine University
St. Cloud State University
Texas State University
Tuskegee University
University of Akron
University of Alabama
University of Alabama at Birmingham
University of Arkansas at Little Rock
University of Central Florida
University of Central Missouri
University of Central Oklahoma
University of Cincinnati
University of Connecticut
University of Dayton

JOYCE JOHNSON

University of Georgia
University of Houston
University of Louisville
University of Missouri
University of Nebraska at Kearney
University of New Hampshire
University of New Haven
University of North Alabama
University of North Carolina: Kenan-Flagler Business School
University of Southern Mississippi
University of Texas at Arlington
University of Texas at Dallas
University of Toledo
University of Texas at Dallas
University of Toledo

University of Washington
University of Wisconsin –Eau Claire
University of Wisconsin Oshkosh
University of Wisconsin – River Falls
Virginia Tech University
Washington State University
Weber State University
West Virginia University
Western Carolina University
Western Kentucky University
Western Michigan University
Widener University
William Paterson University
Winona State University
Xavier University of Louisiana

ABOUT THE AUTHOR

Joyce Johnson has worked as a sales leader, business consultant, and mentored for over 20 years. Joyce began her career in professional sports and later entered the telecommunications industry leading to a role as Sales Director in Global markets.

Passionate about mentorship and development of college students, this book is a result of her continued commitment to coach students on personal growth and development of their career path. Joyce continues that effort in her role as Vice President of Development, National Sales Network Houston Chapter.

At a young age growing up in Galveston, Texas, she learned to serve others. Joyce has held several board positions; including Chairman of the Board for the Galveston County Gulf Coast Black Nurses Association, COO for the National Basketball Retired Players Association Miami, Founding member of the East Palo Alto Children's Foundation, the Bahamas Sports Foundation, and served many others.

JOYCE **JOHNSON**

She is a graduate of the historical Prairie View A&M University where she received a BA in Communications. She also pledged the undergraduate chapter of Alpha Kappa Alpha Sorority, Inc. Joyce completed her graduate studies obtaining an MBA in Global Management from the University of Phoenix.

www.ingramcontent.com/pod-product-compliance
Lightning Source LLC
Chambersburg PA
CBHW050118230526
45470CB00004B/1891